ELMHURST PUBLIC LIBRARY

3 1135 02018 3080

LITTLE EXPLORER

MAMMALS

A 4D BOOK

by Jaclyn Jaycox

ELMHURST PUBLIC LIBRARY
125 S. Prospect Avenue
Elmhurst, IL 60126-3298

PEBBLE
a capstone imprint

Download the Capstone 4D app!

- Ask an adult to download the Capstone 4D app.

- Scan the cover and stars inside the book for additional content.

When you scan a spread, you'll find fun extra stuff to go with this book! You can also find these things on the web at www.capstone4D.com using the password: mammals.26462

Little Explorer is published by Pebble,
1710 Roe Crest Drive, North Mankato, Minnesota 56003
www.mycapstone.com

Copyright © 2019 by Pebble, a Capstone imprint.
All rights reserved. No part of this publication may be reproduced in whole or in part, or stored in a retrieval system, or transmitted in any form or by any means, electronic, mechanical, photocopying, recording, or otherwise, without written permission of the publisher.

The name of the Smithsonian Institution and the sunburst logo are registered trademarks of the Smithsonian Institution. For more information, please visit www.si.edu.

Library of Congress Cataloging-in-Publication Data
Names: Jaycox, Jaclyn, 1983– author.
Title: Mammals : a 4D book / by Jaclyn Jaycox.
Description: North Mankato, Minnesota : an imprint of Pebble, [2019] | Series: Smithsonian little explorer. Little zoologist | Audience: Age 4–8. Identifiers: LCCN 2018004127 (print) | LCCN 2018009134 (ebook) | ISBN 9781543526585 (eBook PDF) | ISBN 9781543526462 (hardcover) | ISBN 9781543526523 (paperback) Subjects: LCSH: Mammals—Juvenile literature.
Classification: LCC QL706.2 (ebook) | LCC QL706.2 .J39 2019 (print) | DDC 599—dc23
LC record available at https://lccn.loc.gov/2018004127

Editorial Credits

Michelle Hasselius, editor; Kazuko Collins, designer;
Svetlana Zhurkin, media researcher;
Kris Wilfahrt, production specialist

Our very special thanks to Jen Zoon, communications specialist at Smithsonian's National Zoo, for her review. Capstone would also like to thank Kealy Gordon, Product Development Manager, and the following at Smithsonian Enterprises: Ellen Nanney, Licensing Manager; Brigid Ferraro, Vice President, Education and Consumer Products; and Carol LeBlanc, Senior Vice President, Education and Consumer Products.

Image Credits
Alamy: Ganesh H Shankar, 24; Newscom: WENN/ZOB/CB2, 20; Shutterstock: Andrei Medvedev, 6, Andrew M. Allport, 14, Artur Janichev, 5 (top left), bakdc, 4, bluehand, 8, Bryan Brazil, 28, David C Azor, 22, Don Mammoser, 17, Edwin Butter, 5 (bottom middle), 15, Eric Gevaert, cover, Eric Isselee, 2–3, graja, 19, Hung Chung Chih, 21, John A. Anderson, 5 (bottom left), Joost van Uffelen, 10, Karla Wilson, 5 (bottom right), Katesalin Pagkaihang, 1, Leonardo Mercon, 27, Leonid Smirnov, 29, LeonP, 23 (back), Marek Velechovsky, 13, Martin Mecnarowski, 25, Mauricio S Ferreira, 5 (top middle), Moarly, 11, Nagel Photography, 12, Nantawat Chotsuwan, 5 (top right), paula french, 7 (bottom), Radovan Zierik, 23 (inset), Rosa Jay, 26 (right), Uwe Bergwitz, 26 (left), Vladislav T. Jirousek, 18, Wendy Townrow, 9; Smithsonian's National Zoo: Photo courtesy of Baton Rouge Zoo, 7 (top); Svetlana Zhurkin, 16

Design Elements by Shutterstock

Printed and bound in the United States.
PA021

TABLE OF CONTENTS

J
599
Jay

The Smithsonian's National Zoo is located in Washington, D.C. Founded in 1889, it's one of the oldest zoos in the United States. About 2 million visitors come each year to see animals from all around the world. The Zoo is home to about 1,800 animals. This includes 83 different species of mammals. Zoologists and keepers take care of and study the animals at the Zoo.

ANIMAL CLASSES

Scientists place animals into six main classes, or groups. This makes it easier for scientists to study them.

amphibians

birds

fish

invertebrates

mammals

reptiles

In 1974 the Smithsonian Conservation Biology Institute was founded. Here, scientists study endangered species and their habitats. Scientists use what they learn to help save animals from becoming extinct.

ASIAN ELEPHANT

Asian elephants are some of the largest land mammals in the world. These huge animals weigh between 3 and 6 tons. They grow 6 to 12 feet (1.8 to 3.8 meters) tall.

Asian elephants are found in forests in India and Southeast Asia. They mostly eat grass. They also eat roots, bark, leaves, and fruit. There are seven Asian elephants in the Zoo's Elephant Trails exhibit—Ambika, Shanthi, Bozie, Kamala, Maharani, Swarna, and Spike.

MEET THE ELEPHANTS

Ambika—Ambika has lived at the Zoo since 1961. She is 70 years old. Ambika likes to be around other elephants and people.

Shanthi—Shanthi has been at the Zoo since 1976. She likes to play music. Keepers give her harmonicas, horns, and other noisemakers to play with.

Bozie—Bozie arrived at the Zoo in 2013. When she gets excited, Bozie squeaks, honks, and uses her trunk to make trumpet sounds.

Bozie

Kamala—Kamala came to the Zoo in 2014 with her daughter, Maharani. She seems to enjoy the smell of feet! Kamala will rumble and squeak when she sees and smells them. These sounds tell keepers she is happy and excited.

Maharani—Nicknamed "Rani," Maharani loves getting attention from the keepers and other elephants. She looks to her mom, Kamala, for direction when faced with something new.

Swarna—Swarna came to the Zoo in 2014. She is the smallest elephant at the Zoo, but she has a big personality.

Spike—Spike came to the Zoo on March 23, 2018. He weighs about 6.5 tons. Spike has a laid-back and calm personality.

There are no bones in an elephant's trunk. But it has about 150,000 muscles and tendons.

ASIAN SMALL-CLAWED OTTER

Asian small-clawed otters are the smallest otter species. These little mammals weigh less than 10 pounds (4.5 kilograms). They are up to 2 feet (0.6 m) long. They live in streams and rivers in southern China, Southeast Asia, Indonesia, and the Philippines. They eat crabs, fish, insects, and snails.

A family of Asian small-clawed otters live at the Zoo. Chowder and his three pups—Peaches, Rutabaga, and Kevin—can be found in the Asia Trail exhibit. Keepers feed them fish, kibble, crabs, mussels, clams, mealworms, and crayfish.

Asian small-clawed otters can close their ears and nostrils while swimming underwater.

Asian small-clawed otters live in family groups of 15 to 20 otters. But they hunt alone.

CALIFORNIA SEA LION

California sea lions live along the coast of western North America, in the Pacific Ocean. They are about 8 feet (2.4 m) long. They weigh up to 600 pounds (272 kg).

Sea lions are social animals. They gather in groups called rookeries during breeding season.

California sea lions will stick their flippers in the water when it's hot outside. They also throw sand on their backs to cool off.

There are five sea lions at the Zoo. A female sea lion named Catalina was born in June 2016.

California sea lions are fast swimmers. They can swim up to 30 miles (48 kilometers) per hour. They are also excellent hunters. Sea lions eat fish and squid. At the Zoo's American Trail exhibit, they eat thawed frozen squid, herring, butterfish, capelin, and mackerel.

Dama gazelles are the largest gazelle species. They are about 3 feet (0.9 m) tall at the shoulders. They weigh between 88 and 190 pounds (40 to 86 kg).

Dama gazelles are critically endangered—less than 400 live in the wild. They live in the desert regions of Chad and Sudan. Dama gazelles eat desert shrubs and grasses. There are four dama gazelles at the Zoo—Adara, Fahima, Zafirah, and Edem. They can be found in the Cheetah Conservation Station.

Dama gazelles can live to be 19 years old in zoos.

Golden lion tamarins are small monkeys known for their reddish-gold coats. They are found in Brazil, living in canopies in the rain forest. The canopies are made from tree branches and leaves high above the rain forest floor. Golden lion tamarins are only 6 to 10 inches (15 to 25 centimeters) long. They weigh up to 2 pounds (0.9 kg).

Golden lion tamarins are an endangered species. There are only about 3,200 left in the wild.

Golden lion tamarins eat fruits, insects, and small invertebrates. They are fed carrots, sweet potatoes, green beans, hard-boiled eggs, mealworms, and crickets. They can be seen in the Small Mammal House.

ORANGUTAN

Orangutans are the largest mammals that live in trees. Males can weigh up to 220 pounds (100 kg). Orangutans are found in forests in Borneo and Sumatra. They eat fruits, leaves, and other plants.

Orangutan means *person of the forest.*

Sumatran orangutan

There are three species of orangutans—Sumatran, Bornean, and Tapanuli.

"Each of our gorillas and orangutans receive a few nutritious biscuits in the morning as part of their daily breakfast. . . . While the apes nosh, keepers gauge the animals' appetites and closely examine them for any cuts, scrapes, or health issues that need to be addressed."

—Melba Brown, animal keeper

Orangutans' strong, long arms make them well suited for life in the trees. They climb, walk, sway, and swing to get around. The Zoo has seven orangutans—Kiko, Kyle, Lucy, Bonnie, Iris, Batang, and Redd. They can be found in the Great Ape House and Think Tank exhibits.

PATAGONIAN MARA

Patagonian maras have long ears like rabbits, but their small bodies look similar to tiny deer. These rodents are found in grasslands in central and southern Argentina. They are 27.5 inches (70 cm) long and weigh up to 35 pounds (16 kg).

Patagonian maras travel in pairs. Males protect their mates from predators.

There are three adult maras at the Zoo—Maggie, Michonne, and Jesus.

Patagonian maras can walk, hop, gallop, or bounce on all four legs. They are great runners, reaching speeds of 28 miles (45 km) per hour. At the Zoo, keepers feed them fruits, vegetables, nuts, and hay. They are located near the Great Cats exhibit.

RED PANDA

Red pandas live in high forests and mountains in Asia. They weigh up to 13 pounds. They are 22 to 24 inches (56 to 62 cm) long. Red pandas are expert climbers. They use trees for shelter, to escape predators, and to sunbathe in the winter. Red pandas eat bamboo. They also eat fruits, insects, and plant roots.

At the Zoo, red pandas eat biscuits, grapes, chopped apples, and bananas. There are three red pandas living at the Smithsonian's National Zoo—Asa, Nutmeg, and Jackie. They live together in the Asia Trail exhibit.

Since 1962 more than 100 red panda cubs have been born at the Smithsonian's National Zoo and Conservation Biology Institute.

Red pandas are endangered. There may be fewer than 2,500 red pandas in the wild.

Ring-tailed lemurs get their name from the black and white rings around their tails. These endangered mammals live in forests and open, dry areas in southwestern Madagascar. Adult lemurs weigh about 6 pounds (3 kg). Their tails are up to 2 feet (61 cm) long.

Lemurs communicate with each other using facial expressions and alarm calls. When they are in danger, they will make a noise that starts as a grunt and turns into a bark. This warns the other lemurs in their group.

There are four male ring-tailed lemurs at the Zoo—Southside Johnny, Tom Petty, Bowie, and Birch.

Ring-tailed lemurs that live at the Zoo love to eat fruit.

Ring-tailed lemurs spend most of their day looking for food. They eat leaves, insects, and flowers.

SLOTH BEAR

Sloth bears are not your average bears. They eat termites, ants, fruits, and flowers. Sloth bears will stick their snouts into nests or holes and suck up the insects. Sloth bears can be 6 feet (1.8 m) long. They weigh up to 300 pounds (136 kg). They are found in forests and grasslands in India, Sri Lanka, and southern Nepal.

Sloth bear mothers carry their cubs on their backs.

Sloth bears are noisy. They snort and grunt while searching for food.

Remi's favorite treats are apple slices.

The Smithsonian's National Zoo is home to two sloth bears—Niko and Remi. Niko and Remi have indoor and outdoor habitats at the Asia Trail exhibit. People who can't visit the Zoo can watch these sloth bears online on the Zoo's webcam.

Southern tamanduas are found in South America. They live in rain forests, mangroves, savannahs, and near streams and rivers. Tamanduas use their long, sticky tongues to scoop up insects. Their tongues can be as long as 15.7 inches (40 cm). Southern tamanduas spend most of their time in trees, eating ants, termites, and bees. They weigh about 10 pounds (4.5 kg).

Southern tamanduas have huge claws to rip apart logs in search for food. They also use their claws to protect themselves from predators.

Southern tamanduas have no fur on the underside of their tails. This helps them grip tree branches.

There are two southern tamanduas at the Zoo—Manny and Cayenne.

Sumatran tigers are found only on the island of Sumatra. It is estimated that there are fewer than 400 Sumatran tigers living in the wild.

At the Zoo, tigers are given rabbits to eat to keep their teeth healthy and exercise their jaw muscles.

No two tigers have the same stripe pattern on their coats.

Sumatran tigers are the smallest tiger species. Males weigh up to 310 pounds (141 kg). Females weigh about 200 pounds (91 kg). Sumatran tigers eat meat, such as wild boar and deer. At the Zoo, keepers feed them ground beef. There is one Sumatran tiger in the Great Cats exhibit, a female named Damai. She had a cub in July 2017. The cub moved to the San Diego Zoo in September.

GLOSSARY

canopy—the middle layer of the rain forest where the greenery is thick and there is little sunlight

communicate—to pass along thoughts, feelings, or information

endangered—at risk of dying out

exhibit—a display that usually includes objects and information to show and tell people about a certain subject

extinct—no longer living; an extinct animal is one that has died out, with no more of its kind

flipper—an armlike body part that an ocean or freshwater animal uses to swim

gallop—to run so fast that all four legs leave the ground at once

grassland—large area of wild grasses

habitat—the natural place and conditions in which a plant or animal lives

mammal—a warm-blooded animal that breathes air and has hair or fur; female mammals feed milk to their young

mate—the male or female partner of a pair of animals

nostril—one of the two outside openings in the nose used to breathe and smell

predator—an animal that hunts other animals for food

rain forest—a large, open area where grass and low plants grow

snout—the long front part of an animal's head; it includes the nose, mouth, and jaws

species—a group of plants or animals that have the same ancestor and share common characteristics

tendon—a strong band of tissue that attaches muscles to bones

trunk—the elephant's long nose and upper lip

CRITICAL THINKING QUESTIONS

1. What is the difference between Asian elephants and African elephants?

2. How do California sea lions keep cool? Use the text to help you with your answer.

3. Explore the Smithsonian's website. What animals can be seen on webcams?

READ MORE

Gagne, Tammy. *Sloth Bears.* Wild Bears. Mankato, Minn.: Amicus High Interest, 2016.

Gregory, Josh. *Red Pandas.* Nature's Children. New York: Children's Press, 2017.

Riehecky, Janet. *Orangutans.* Endangered and Threatened Animals. North Mankato, Minn.: Capstone Press, 2013.

INTERNET SITES

Use FactHound to find Internet sites related to this book.

Visit www.facthound.com

Just type in 9781543526462 and go.

Super-cool stuff! Check out projects, games and lots more at **www.capstonekids.com**

31

INDEX